Atlantis and the Atlanteans

(The Emerald Tablets and Other Texts)

Anna Zubkova, Mikhail Nikolenko,
Maria Shtil, Larisa Vavulina,
Vladimir Antonov

Edited by
Vladimir Antonov

Translated from Russian by
Mikhail Nikolenko

2008

ISBN 978-1438217604

Published in 2008 by CreateSpace

This book provides information about the spiritual life in Atlantis. It includes, in particular, excerpts from conversations with the former Atlanteans, who worked and developed during their incarnations on that continent.

The main value of the book is a description of the methodology of spiritual development.

This book is intended primarily for those who seek the way to achieving the spiritual Perfection.

www.atlantis-and-atlanteans.org
www.swami-center.org

© Vladimir Antonov, 2008.

Contents

THE EMERALD TABLETS OF THOTH-THE-ATLANTEAN 6

THE EMERALD TABLET OF HERMES TRISMEGISTUS 14

ADLER 16

THOTH-THE-ATLANTEAN 29

CAIRO 39

NIKIFOR 44

ODIN 50

BIBLIOGRAPHY 56

"I began preaching to people the beauty of religion and knowledge.

"O people, men born on the Earth, who indulge in drunkenness, sleep, and the ignorance of God! Sober up, cease your surfeit, awake from your dullness!

"Why do you give up yourselves to death while you have power to partake of immortality?

"Depart from dark path, be partakers of immortality, abandon forever your vices!

"Nowhere but in God can you find good!"

(From Hermes'[1] address to the Egyptians)

Atlantis was an archipelago consisting of two large islands situated in the Atlantic Ocean near the Mediterranean Sea. There existed the highly developed civilization of the Atlanteans. The most important point about this civilization is that it possessed the true religious-philosophical knowledge, which allowed many people to advance quickly in their development — to the Divine level — and accomplish thus their personal human evolution.

However, with time the Atlantis' spiritual culture degraded, and, as a result, the power in the country was taken over by aggressive people, who preferred black magic and domination over others rather than the principle of the true spiritual development. Then God made the islands of Atlantis sink into the ocean.

---

[1] Hermes Trismegistus is a name of Thoth-the-Atlantean in His next incarnation in Egypt.

But the higher spiritual knowledge was preserved by some Atlanteans, Who achieved Divinity. They brought it into Egypt and other countries, where this knowledge existed for some time providing a basis for the local spiritual culture.

The Emerald Tablets of Thoth-the-Atlantean[2]

In the *Emerald Tablets*, Thoth-the-Atlantean explains the reason for the destruction of Atlantis: confidential knowledge was imparted to unworthy people and the latter began using it for evil purposes. They adopted also bloody sacrifices — and this resulted in numerous incarnations of hellish beings among people.

When the destruction of Atlantis happened (two islands submerged into the ocean one after another according to the Divine Will), Thoth-the-Atlantean moved to Egypt (Khem) with a group of other Divine Atlanteans.

The *Primordial*[3] advised Thoth thus: "Go forth as a Teacher of men! Go forth preserving the records (with Teachings) until in time the *Light* grows among men!

"*Light*[4] shall You be all through the ages, hidden yet found by enlightened men.

---

[2] This chapter presents a selection of excerpts (compiled and edited by Dr.V.Antonov) from the book of Divine Thoth-the-Atlantean discovered by Dr.M.Doreal in his expedition to the pyramids in South America.

[3] The Primordial Consciousness, the Creator, God-the-Father, Jehovah, Allah, Tao, Svarog, and other names used in different languages — all these are synonyms.

[4] *Light* is not a symbol but a real state of the Divine Consciousness.

"For working on all the Earth, give We You power, free You to give it to others or take it away."

And then Thoth worked as a *Representative of the Primordial*.

… Thoth relates that He went the entire Path to Mergence with the *Primordial*. He writes that anyone can traverse this Path. The Path necessarily contains obstacles, which create difficulties for travelers: these difficulties prevent the weak, ethically unworthy, or intellectually immature people from going further. "Go! But do not take with you the unwise, insincere, weak!" says Thoth.

Thoth gives basic recommendations for initial harmonization of the chakra system. For fulfilling just these recommendations He promises health and longevity.[5]

On the higher stages of meditative practices one has to dive with the consciousness into the *Depths* of the multidimensional space and cognize there "star worlds" and the *Light* of the *Great Fire* on the Path to the Abode of the *Primordial*[6]. There are also other spatial dimensions, which are "vacant to all seeming, yet hidden within them are the *keys*…"[7]

Thoth also explains one of the higher meditations — the *Temple* and its particular variation — the *Pyramid*.

---

[5] See information about the chakras and methods of working with them in [2].

[6] The Primordial Consciousness; synonyms: the Creator, God-the-Father, Jehovah, Allah, Tao, Svarog and other terms in different languages.

[7] These "spaces" are really existing spatial dimensions (planes, eons, lokas) that can be cognized by a developed consciousness. They are represented on the scheme for studying the structure of the Absolute published in [2].

About the history of His own spiritual ascent Thoth says the following:

"Once in a time long forgotten, I, Thoth, opened the *doorway*, penetrated into other spaces and learned of the secrets concealed.

"Often did I journey down the dark pathway unto the space where the *Light* ever glows.

"Long then dwelt I in the Temple of the *Primordial* until at last I was One with the *Light*."

Later Thoth incarnated again in Egypt as Hermes Trismegistus (Thrice-born[8]).

* * *

Thoth gives the following directions to spiritual seekers:

Preserve and keep the command of the *Primordial*:

Look in your life for disorder and get rid of it! Balance and order your life!

Quell all the chaos of emotions and you shall have harmony in life.[9]

Conquer by silence the bondage of words.

Keep ever your eyes on the *Light*!

Surely when you deserve it, you shall be *one* with your Master! And surely then you shall be *one with the All*[10]!

---

[8] See explanation in the Gospel of Philip in [1].

[9] There has to remain only the emotions of love on the background of inner quietness — *hesychia*.

[10] By *All* or *Whole* here and further in the text Thoth means God in the aspect of Absolute.

Know My commandments! Keep them and fulfill them, and I will be with you, helping and guiding you into the *Light*!

Out of the darkness shall you rise upward, *one* with the *Light*!

Man has to strive to become the *Divine Sun*[11].

Follow this Path and you shall be *One* with the *All*!

Light comes only to him who strives. Hard is the Pathway that leads to the Wisdom, hard is the Pathway that leads to the *Light*. Many shall you find the stones in your pathway: many the mountains to climb toward the *Light*.

Man, know that always beside you walk the *Messengers of Light*. Open to all is Their Pathway, to all who are ready to walk into the *Light*!

Suns are They, *Messengers of Light* to shine among men. Like man are They and yet are unlike.

Know that many dark shadows shall fall on your *light*[12] striving to quench with the shadows of darkness the *light* of the soul that strives to be free. Many the pitfalls that lie on this Way. Seek ever to gain Greater Wisdom! Cognize — you shall know the Light!

Light is eternal and darkness is fleeting. Seek ever, O man, for the *Light*! Know ever that as *Light* fills your being, darkness for you shall soon disappear!

Open the soul to the *Messengers of Light*! Let Them enter and fill you with Light!

Keep ever your face to this Goal!

---

[11] This is one of the final meditations on the spiritual Path.

[12] Light appearing in the spiritual heart when a soul begins to walk the spiritual Path.

... Open the soul, O man, to the *cosmos* and let it "flow" through you as one with the soul![13]

Man's evolution consists in the process of changing to forms that are not of this world. Grows he in time to the *formless* — to live on a higher plane. Know that you must become *formless* before you can be one with the *Light*.

Listen, O man, to My voice, telling of pathways to *Light*, showing the way of attainment: how you shall become *one* with the *Light*:

Search first the mysteries of *Earth's Heart*! Seek the *Flame*[14] *of the Living Earth*! Bathe in the glare of this *Flame*!

Know, O man, you are complex, a being of matter and of *Fire*. Let your *Flame*[15] shine out brightly! Be you only the *Flame*!

Seek ever more Wisdom! Find it in the *Heart of the Flame*! Know that only by your striving can *Light* pour into you!

Only the one, who of *Light* has the fullest, can hope to pass by the guards of the Way, who prevent unworthy people from entering it.

You shall cognize yourself as *Light* and make yourself ready to pass on the Way.

---

[13] This can be achieved only by means of work with the *spiritual heart*.

[14] *Flame* or *Divine Fire* is one of the states of the Divine Consciousness. This is also described in the Teachings of Agni yoga.

[15] This statement concerns the Atmic component of the human multidimensional organism. On the Path of the spiritual growth man has to cognize himself as Atman and then to merge with the Paramatman. Two latter concepts are denoted also as *Higher Self*.

Wisdom is hidden in darkness. When shining with *Soul-Flame*, find you the Wisdom, then shall you be born again as *Light,* and then shall you become the *Divine Sun*.[16]

Grow into *One* with the *Light!* Be a channel of Divine Principles to the world of men!

Seek, O man, to find the great Pathway that leads to eternal Life — through the image of the *Divine Sun!*

… Know, O man, you are only a soul! The body is nothing! The soul is everything! Let not your body be a fetter!

Cast off the darkness and travel in *Light!* Learn to cast off your body, O man, and be free from it![17] Become the true *Light* and unite then with the *Great Light!*[18]

Know that throughout the space the eternal and infinite *Consciousness* exists. Though from superficial knowledge It is hidden, yet still forever exists.

The key to these Higher worlds is *within* you; it can be found only *within*.[19]

Open the *gateway* within you, and surely you, too, shall *live* the true life!

… Man, you think that you live… but know that you former life can lead you only to death. For as long

---

[16] This constitutes the second and third *Births*.

[17] This can be realized correctly only through the work on developing oneself as a spiritual heart. If one tries to perform it in other way, such a person comes to coarse spatial dimensions. How to "open" and develop the spiritual heart is shown and explained in detail in our video film *Spiritual Heart* and in our other films and books.

[18] I.e., Atman, which is one with Paramatman.

[19] Within the developed spiritual heart.

as you are bound to your body, no true life exists for you! Only the soul which is free from the material world has life which is really true life! All else is only a bondage, a fetter from which to be free!

Think not that man is born for the earthly! Though born on the Earth, he is a light-like spirit! Yet, without true knowledge he can never become free!

... Darkness surrounds the souls seeking to be born in *Light*. Darkness fetters souls... Only the one who is seeking may ever hope for Freedom!

Let you be the *Divine Sun of the Great Light*! Fulfill this and you shall be free!

The Great Light that fills all the Cosmos is willing to help you, O man! Make you of your body a *torch of Light* that shall shine among men!

... Hear and understand: the *Flame* is the source of all things; all things are its manifestation!

Seek to be *One* with the *Divine Sun*!

Hold your thought on uniting the *Light* with your human body.

Light is the Source of all the life; for without the *Great Light* nothing can ever exist!

Know, *Light* is the basis of all formed matter.

Know, O man, that all space is filled by worlds within worlds.

Deep beneath the *image of Pyramid* lies My secret. Seek and find in the *Pyramid* I built.

Follow this *key* I left for you. Seek and the doorway to the true *Life* shall be yours! Seek in My *Pyramid* deep beneath it, and in the *Wall*.[20]

---

[20] This concerns the higher stages of meditative practice.

Know that it is in the *Pyramid* I built that shall you find the secret way into the *true Life*.

… Seek and find there That which I have hidden! There shall you find the "underground entrance" to the secrets hidden before you were men.

Know We that of all, nothing else matters excepting the growth one can gain with the soul. Know We the flesh is fleeting. The things men count great are nothing to Us. The things We expect from you are not of your bodies but are only the perfected state of the souls.

When you can learn that nothing but progress of the soul can count in the end, then truly you are free from all bondage, free to work in accordance with your predestination!

Know, O man, you are to aim at Perfection, for only thus can you attain to the Goal!

Know that the future is never in fixation but follows man's free will! Man can only "read the future" through the causes that bring the effects in destinies.

Know that your body when in perfect balance may never be touched by the finger of death! Aye, even "accident" may only approach when you abandon your predestination! When you are in harmony with your predestination, you shall live on in time and not taste of death.

… Know you not that in the *Earth's Heart* is the source of harmony of all things that exist and have being on its face? By the soul you are connected with the *Earth's Heart*, and by your flesh — with the matter of *Earth*.

When you have learned to maintain harmony in yourself, then shall you draw on from the *harmony of the Earth's Heart.* Exist then shall you while Earth is existing, changing in form, only when Earth, too, shall change: tasting not of death, but one with this planet, living in your body till all pass away.

... Three are the qualities of God in His *Light-Home*[21]: Infinite Power, Infinite Wisdom, Infinite Love.

Three are the powers given to spiritual Masters: to transmute evil, to assist good, to use discrimination[22].

Three are the things They manifest: Power, Wisdom, and Love.

Three are the Manifestations of Spirit creating all things: *Divine Love* possessing the perfect knowledge, *Divine Wisdom* knowing all possible means of helping living beings in their development, Divine Power which is possessed by the *Primordial Consciousness* Whose essence is Divine Love and Wisdom.

Darkness and *Light* are both of one nature, different only in seeming, for each arose from one Source. Darkness is chaos. *Light* is Divine Harmony. Darkness transmuted is *Light*.

This, My children, your purpose in being: transmutation of darkness into *Light!*"

The Emerald Tablet of Hermes Trismegistus

I say here only truth and nothing else!

That which is below is similar to that which is above. And that which is above is similar to that which

---

[21] The Abode of the Creator.
[22] Discrimination of the qualities of souls and determination of the best conditions for their development.

is below. One has to know this in order to gain the cognition of the marvelous *Primordial One!*[23]

Everything material came into existence by the intent of the *Primordial One*. All material objects became manifest through densification of the energy by the *Primordial One*.

The *Sun*[24] is the Father of the manifest world; the "lunar"[25] is its mother. The Holy Spirit "brings up" developing souls; the Earth nurtures them. The Father of all the development in the entire universe is present always and everywhere.

His Power is the Supreme Power! It is supreme to everything else! And It is manifested on the Earth — in Its Omnipotence!

Thus divide: the "earthly" — and the *Fiery*[26], the coarse — and the subtle! Act, at that, with great caution, awe, and understanding!

Become the *Subtlest Fire* — and cognize the *Heavenly!* Thus you achieve the *Mergence*. Then come back to the Earth — and you will perceive the *Subtlest* and will have power to transform effectively the imperfect.

This will mean that you have achieved the glory of *Mergence with the Primordial One* and ridden yourselves of the darkness of ignorance.

---

[23] This concerns one particular meditation of buddhi yoga that allows achieving full Mergence with the Primordial Consciousness.

[24] Divine Sun, the Sun of God. Again this concerns one of the highest meditations of the buddhi yoga.

[25] By "lunar" Hermes calls the substance of the "transmirror" eons — protoprakriti and protopurusha. From the latter, matter and souls are formed (see [2]).

[26] Fiery Manifestations of the Creator.

The Power of the *Primordial One* is present beneath everything: beneath both the subtlest and the coarse — and controls them. It is in this way that the Creation exists. And thanks to this marvelous *connectedness of Everything* the development goes on.

This is why My name is Hermes Thriceborn: for I act in all three planes of existence[27] and possess the wisdom of the entire universe!

Thus I have said everything I wanted to say about the *doing of the Sun*.

Adler

Once in autumn, Pastor Larry and Freddy led us to a meeting with another Representative of the Creator — Divine Adler. We went for a long time along a trail in pine forest suffused with morning mist and songs of birds.

"Adler is the Greatest Teacher. He has been present on the Earth always. You are going to interview Him," They said.

Soon we came to a place where a giant Mahadouble of Adler — hundreds of meters in size — stood over the forest.

We built a fire, warmed ourselves, drank some coffee with sandwiches, rested a little, and then asked Adler to tell about Himself.

He began the narration:

"I never incarnated on the Earth with the purpose of learning for God. I came there being already Divine.

---

[27] In the eons of the Creator, the Holy Spirit, and in the world of matter.

"For the first time, I appeared in a material body on this planet about in the same time as Ushastik described[28], just a little later than He did.

"Later, the main oasis of spiritual culture began to form in the Western Mediterranean."

"Was it Atlantis?"

"Yes. It was the area where the Mediterranean sea is connected with the ocean. Though the form of the coast is completely different now.

"Atlantis was My work: from the very beginning till the end I created the spiritual culture of Atlantis. From there it moved partly to Egypt.

"I took with Me worthy people and led them into Myself — an incarnation after incarnation, a wave after wave. Thus I incarnated there several times.

"In the middle ages, I worked in Europe, living in one body from 14th to 18th century. I could appear and disappear, but always it was one and the same body of Mine."

"Was it You who guided Napoleon?"

"Yes"

"Why he did not manage to liberate Russia from inquisition?"

"The epic work of Napoleon reached a deadlock when he proclaimed himself a king on the Earth, forgetting about the main role of God. There must be Theocracy rather than kingocracy — then everything will be fine!"

"His war against Russia was a mistake?"

---

[28] See [1].

"He made a mistake earlier: when he began to feel himself a king. He had to feel himself a God's messenger."

"Did he feel himself a king from the very beginning?"

"In the beginning, he felt himself a prophet and fulfilled My Will — the Will of the Creator.

"… My last incarnation was in the Netherlands."

"Were You a king?"

"No, but I was at the court. I took on Myself the role of a counselor; not in the narrow meaning of this word, not as a post: I was a confidant of the monarch.

"The history tells about 'immortal' people, i.e. those possessing immortal bodies…"

"Saint Germain?"

"No, this is a legend. But I really lived among people for several centuries in one body."

"Are You incarnate at present?"

"No."

… Adler shows His appearance of the time when He was incarnate:

"In this appearance I came to the Netherlands.

"In the Netherlands at present there are sprouts of spirituality. This is why I direct your attention there. You have to spread the information about Me in this country. In the Netherlands there is a growing generation of promising people; they are about 200 persons — young, brave, strong. Soon they will learn about you with My help.

"… And now I am going to tell you a little more of My history… One cannot find this information in the historical scriptures or in the Internet…

"Yes, there are legends about the 'immortal' in South India, in China, in other countries of South-East Asia, and on the American continent. They were Divine Teachers — the Supervisors of the development of the human civilization. They come to the planet in flesh when it is necessary to correct the direction of the development of souls on the Earth — not the course of events but the direction of the evolution of souls.

"I never took on Myself the role of a prophet or Messiah, who preach to crowds of people. But wherever I came to, in the midst of chaos, darkness, and ignorance, — there appeared the first sparks of light, the first ideas of good, the first thoughts about freedom…

"In this way I would appear and disappear, without attracting much attention to Myself, being a Boundless Consciousness connected with the body which, like a lens, transmitted to the material plane the ideas and thoughts more effectively than they can be transmitted from the non-incarnate state. These ideas fell like raindrops on the dry soil… and it took long time for first shoots to appear…

"Do you want to participate in such work?"

"What does one need for this?"

"One needs to treat the body with the energies of the Creator; one needs the state of Continuum from the Creator. And one needs to achieve the state described by Jesus: 'Every cell of My body became conscious…'

"This requires that the awareness of oneself in the Ocean of the Creator become a constant, unchanging state, and the energies of the material body be replaced with the Divine Energies.

"Then one gains the possibility to live in the material body with full awareness of God. The body serves then as a link between the Creator and His Creation. It becomes similar to a lens or a slit focusing the Ray the Divine Consciousness, Divine Energy — onto the material plane.

"... My work in the medieval Europe in 14th-18th centuries allowed raising slowly the wave of the Renaissance.

"... Very slowly love and freedom ripen in the souls of people. For centuries the drops of Divine Light fell into darkness as if disappearing with no result..., but they produced eventually sprouts...

"It was Me who initiated the wave of Lutheranism, Reformation in Europe: i.e. the ideas about the possibility for man to communicate with God directly, without intermediates, without rituals... France, Germany, the Netherlands... This process was completed with the liberating wave of Napoleon, which washed out almost completely the filth of the inquisition from the Earth.

"The evolution of souls is a slow, gradual process. It is impossible to destroy in an instant the slavery of souls unable to comprehend the ideas of love and freedom. We have told you already about this work of the Divine Teachers; it was described by Vysotin, Rossi, Babaji. One does not need an eternal body for this... Every One of Us performs a part of this work...

"The Representatives of the Father: Jesus, Krishna were prominent figures proclaiming the Truth from God... As for Me, I was unnoticed — like an invisible brush touching the canvas. But the traces left by this brush remained in the history of souls. With My physical body I penetrated to and fro like a needle that makes stitches with a thread of Divine Light, weaving the Ray of God into the picture of the material plane."

"Will You tell us the history of Your lives in more detail?"

"I will tell about this sometime in future. It is quite interesting; one can make many novels of it...

"Now I want you to look at this *from within*: from within Me, not from within yourselves...

"Fill your bodies with a new life — the life of the Higher Self!

"I will lead you to the Goal as one leads by hand.

"Submerge completely into Me — into the Ocean of the Primordial Consciousness! Feel yourselves this Boundless *Light*! This *Light* is everywhere: wherever you may go!"

"And what about the material plane and interactions with it?"

"This is much simpler than you think. A more difficult matter is to dissolve oneself in Me, to merge with Me completely, to move the self-awareness into Me.

"Once you manage to accomplish this, everything becomes easy then: as you can look into Me though you live with your body in the material plane — even so living in Me you can look at the material plane and act in it from Me.

"This is how I worked in centuries, possessing an eternal body on the material plane: I lived on the plane of Spirit, on the other side of the world of matter. The body served as a beacon — to help incarnate people to find the way Home: to the Abode of the Creator. I performed all deeds in secret, staying behind the 'Curtain', without manifesting too much activity on the material plane.

"I was a secret counselor of rulers and great minds. It is from My bottomless 'well' that they drew their knowledge.

"I worked on spiritualizing the humanity from the first generations of people on the Earth. I always brought the Truth and Knowledge about the Creator of the universe."

"Tell us about how You became one with the Creator. You had to learn to become God, hadn't You?"

"Yes I learned, but not here on the Earth.

"It happened in another epoch of the Evolution. In this Kalpa, I have always been a Part of the Ocean of the Creator's Consciousness. Many times He placed Me — as a part of Him — into material bodies. I did not have to go through the whole cycle of evolution in this Kalpa, starting from minerals and plants. I have always remained a Son of the Creator and have never separated Myself from Him.

"You know how difficult is the process of transformation of consciousness in people — from the 'I' of man into the 'I' of God. I would name the reason for this — the 'materialization' of souls — in the sense that the consciousnesses of people are fettered by the material concerns. People have forgotten that man is a soul, first and foremost. Thus people cease to understand their predestination, the meaning of life.

"... The Creator entrusted Me with the task of creation of this planet from the very beginning. Many times I incarnated on this Earth created by Me. I am its Founder, Creator, Guardian — and the Calm of souls who cognize Me. I absorb them, first by manifesting Myself as the Holy Spirit and then as the Creator.

"Do you understand now the 'alignment of powers' on this planet?

"… At present on the Earth there are very few souls deserving higher initiations. And if one starts to teach people in a 'rough-and-ready' manner, then they do not grow strong enough. This leads either to tragedies of souls who desired something above their capabilities or results in perversions of the true knowledge. And you know how it is hard — to restore the true knowledge in its original purity.

"All the profundity of this knowledge is not comprehensible and not needed for the majority of souls living now on the Earth!"

"How can we separate that what should be hidden from the public and that what should be open to everyone? Our books present the knowledge almost in full."

"Your books are written so that they work as filters. They do not become bestsellers; they are accepted by a few out of thousands. And you should not change this principle by doing something 'to please the public'.

"Yet you have to create pure sources of the true knowledge throughout the entire planet; to these sources I will easily bring deserving seekers!

"The realization of this task has started already through the network of your websites, through translation and publication of your books in other languages. This will be followed by publication and distribution of the books and films in many European countries and on the American continents.

"Understand: a powerful emanation of the Energy of the Creator into the world of people happens when you create books, films, websites! This allows the waves of this Light to spread even on those who do not read and do not seek this knowledge yet! Such an influence is gradual; its effect cannot be observed immediately. The ideas and knowledge come through you to the material world, and changes begin to grow. The further process of changes is My task, not yours. Your task is to shine, to give, to direct the Rays of the Divine Consciousness into this world, to bring love, knowledge, beauty! This is a part of the process of forming new Beingness of the Earth; you will learn to see the mechanisms of this process later.

"… There are three stages of Manifestation of the Divine through a human body:

"The first stage is a genius: when a Divine Soul manifests Itself by means of a human body; at that, a small part of the consciousness in the body and the mind of the body are but an instrument in the Divine Hand. This 'instrument' is not aware of its coessentiality with the Creator. It is only a conductor of the Divine Energy into the world of incarnate people.

"The second stage of the Divine Manifestation is a prophet. In this case the part of the consciousness connected with the body is aware of the Creator's Will; it conveys words, knowledge, states of the Divine Consciousness with full awareness and with full understanding; yet this state is not constant. There are periods when this connection with the Primordial Plane is not active.

"And the third stage is the Highest Divine awareness, when every part of the consciousness connected with the body becomes also Divine. Not many people of the Earth managed to achieve this stage. Usually such are Avatars coming to the Earth Who attained the Divinity in the past.

"I want to add that in the non-incarnate state every Divine Soul is equal to the Primordial Consciousness. Such a Soul, having overcome the small part of 'I' which appears when the Divine Energy is projected onto the material plane, merges into the Ocean of the Primordial Consciousness. And in this Ocean, no one is worse or better, higher or lower. There All are United Divine Self!

"But when Divine Teachers work in the Creation from the non-incarnate state, They manifest again Their Divine Individualities. And then one can notice Their differences. Different are Their abilities and skills accumulated in the past; different is the volume of the Consciousness with which a Divine Individuality can act in the Creation. This difference exists in Their activity in the Creation, but in the Abode of the Primordial Consciousness All They are One.

"… Do you remember some esotericists fantasized that God created the Creation 'out of boredom', that only in the Creation He can become 'aware of Himself'? In such absurdities there is an echo of truth that only that Part of the Primordial Consciousness Which went through the entire cycle of the evolution — only such a Part is capable of being the Creator most actively. It is such Parts that become most actively functioning Manifestations of the Primordial Whole, the Creators of new worlds in the universe.

"This is how God lives and evolves!"

"What would You advise us now?"

"The material body has to be placed onto the Primordial plane of Beingness and then immersed into the Ocean of the Primordial Consciousness. Every cell, every atom of the physical body has *in the depth* the Primordial Consciousness. Oneness with It can become the conscious state of every one of you, inside your bodies, in particular.

"The body can be likened to a sprout on the body of the planet. And in your body, as in the body of the Earth, all planes of the multidimensionality are present.

"Whatever adverse the conditions may be, you should never concentrate your attention on them. You should always be the *United We*!

"What is the difference between you and Me? My 'I' never opposes the Creator but remains one with Him. Your task is to move with self-awareness there where there is only the Higher Self.

"In the beginning you have to merge with the harmony of everything around you, including Us. Everything around loves you! Your responsive love leads to Mergence. And in the mutual love with the Absolute the lower self dissolves.

"I am present in everything and in everyone! From the *Depths*, I manifest everything, control everything, and give the freedom of will to all!

"You live here with the purpose of cognizing the *Oneness*! One can cognize the *Oneness* only by means of living in body in the incarnate state.

"The supreme joy of the soul is Mergence with the Creator. There is no joy above this!

"You live in this world with the purpose of growing into Me! You live there with the purpose of bringing this knowledge to people!

"And let every one of your become aware that he or she has not much time left for Me, for life on the Earth, for realization of that what I have said about — there is very little time left!

"As a powerful whirlpool draws one into its depth, and there is no way to return then, to rise again to the light — even so old age comes unnoticed and destroys people.

"But the warrior of spirit has to have a strong mind and a strong, healthy body.

"Don't you think that everything I have told you is true?

"Every one of you must make his or her contribution to the realization of everything I said about!

"Otherwise... The time will come when it will be raining all the day, leaves will fall from trees, snow will fall... And it may happen that I will say that now it is too late to achieve the Goal... too late! Autumn is old age..."

* * *

"How can one help those who do not withstand the speed of advancement or the trials of the Straight Path?"

"Understand that no one is left without My help! And no one is depraved of My love! I just give every person that which is most appropriate to him or her at the moment. Diseases, other difficulties, loneliness are My lessons that will help souls to realize their mistakes and purify themselves.

"I took people away from you not only for the sake of your successful advancement but also for their own good, for their proper evolution.

"It is good that the fullness of the Divine awareness will come to them in the next incarnation (providing that it will be successful, of course)! I will incarnate these souls in the time and place I need, and through this I will create new waves of the awakening of Truth in the souls of people on the Earth.

"Realize also the fact that the people whom you are thinking about now, having received the spiritual knowledge refused to serve Me in all fullness when I asked them to do so. It would be good if they will serve so in their future lives — and through this will merge into the *United We*.

"… I am everything! Learn to see Me in every manifestation! Everything coming to you is My Will, the manifestation of My Laws!

"Your destiny is in My Hands… What more do you want?

"Resign yourself — and My Power will come to the world through you!

"Resign yourself — and you will accept death as I will command you to accept!

"Resign yourself — and you will accept life as I will send it to you!

"Resign yourself — and the foreordained will happen!

"Resign yourself — and My Joy will come to the world through you!

"Resign yourself — and My Tenderness will come to the world through you!

"Resign yourself — and My Love will come to the world through you!

"Only after you have realized and fulfilled this, will I give you the power to change inevitable, to perform impossible!"[29]

---

[29] Adler talks about resigning oneself to the Will of God and not to the vicious desires of demonic people.

Thoth-the-Atlantean

"How do people start seeking Me? They stretch their arms to the sky and ask Me to enter as *Light* into them. In the same way I began working with you long ago. Recall the meditations *awakening, latihan, spontaneous dance...* It was Me who gave them to you! I became interested in you, Vladimir, at that time already!

"In this way, gradually, young shoots grew on the good soil prepared by Me for you. Other shoots appeared around; some of them withered...

"By now you have formed a group of mature and able souls, and I begin to make the *New Atlanteans* of you! You may call yourselves so!

"Living in *quietness* became habitual for every one of you. I want you to realize that without this quality one cannot advance on the spiritual Path with great strides as you did.

"I bless you to continue your service to God! Receive My Love!"

"Tell us, do You have an immortal body as Adler does?"

"Yes, but it is not intended for incarnations on this continent. I recreate it from time to time among the Indians of North America."

"Is your body of Indian appearance?"

"The genotype of the body is not important, but the molecular structure is restored as it was.

"I visit that region quite often: I recreate the body for a short time — for a week, for ten days, for two

---

Though, even through such people God manifests sometimes His Will.
One has to learn to discriminate it.

days. I visit Indians with the purpose of telling them something."

"Do those Indians live aloof — not in cities?"

"Yes, they live in reservations."

"Why do You prefer that nation?"

"I did not mean anything like that. Every One of Us has no attachments to a particular nation. The choice is always dictated by the necessity against the background of Love for all."

"Are there any mature (for receiving the higher knowledge) souls?"

Thoth shows a typical natural way of life of Indians: they live beside a lake; in evenings they sing tribal hymns specific to this land.

"These people are always in search for personal freedom. This tradition survived through centuries: seeking personal freedom — for oneself, for one's tribe, for all people of the Earth! The problem is — how to tell other people about this?"

Thoth shows an image of a tribe of about 800 people; some of them, including the chief, sit around a fire.

"They sit like you are doing now and listen to Me.

"I am always an Honored Guest among them.

"Indians can tell much to other people of the Earth. Unfortunately almost no one listens to them.

"… At present I can impart My knowledge in full to no one but to you. The broadness of the world outlook, the deepness of the cognition of Me are most full in your case.

"This is why I entrusted you with the task of spiritual service on the Earth on behalf of Me.

"Every step in this important work has to be taken with My help, with the help of every One of Us. Realize the profound importance of this stage of your service on the Earth! You bear an enormous responsibility! And everything that you do has to be done responsibly, solemnly, and earnestly!

"Recall Atlantis. Now God sends to the Earth a similar project — restoration of ancient knowledge, the knowledge of the Atlanteans — through you, My dear! To Me, you are My small Atlantis!

"The intention of the Creator is to fill, to impregnate the people of the Earth with this knowledge — like a flooding river in spring!

"I suggest that you be constantly aware of your responsibility and of the importance of this task — the restoration of the ancient spiritual knowledge originating directly from the Creator!"

"Thoth, tell us please about Your life in Atlantis!"

"It was long ago, at the dawn of the civilization; modern people know almost nothing about this time.

"Atlantis! My beautiful Atlantis — My native land, where I was born and grew up!

"In that time, on the islands of Atlantis there lived a well advanced civilization. They had, for example, a system of water supply in buildings.

"The Atlanteans possessed also the true knowledge about the meaning of life: about advancement to God, to the Common Divine Source. The life of their society was based on these ideas. Teaching about the structure of the universe and the place of man in it, about how people's destinies are formed and about the right way of living — all it was a natural, integral part of their educational system.

"The spiritual life of the Atlantean society was guided by highest initiates; they were conveyors of truths from God.

"The inhabitants of Atlantis were not gods but ordinary people, and their life was not carefree. Like other nations on the Earth they had to 'plough and sow'. And they had most of the problems that any human society has.

"But the main virtue of the Atlantean civilization was the teachings about the true purpose of life accepted by the society as fundamental. And though the Atlanteans were mere mortals, there was a truly Divine component in their lives and views.

"... My learning began in one of the Atlantis' spiritual schools. A very young man, I just began to discover for Myself this wonderful world.

"The process of initial learning took years. The students had to master, first of all, the basic skills of psychic self-regulation — i.e. the control of one's own emotional states. In addition, they received broad theoretical material.

"This initial stage of learning was open almost for everyone, contrary to the higher stages. With the end of this stage, the majority of the students quitted the school; only a few were selected by the tutors for further learning. Thus the initial course served also the second purpose: with its help the tutors could find among many people promising souls capable of advancing further.

"I was one of such students: a young man striving for the higher levels of spiritual development demonstrated the leaders of our society.

"But the selection for this learning was very strict. The aspirants were necessarily tested for steadfastness, resoluteness in their decision to go this Path. This testing period could last for years: until the aspirant proves, in the opinion of the tutors, the strength of his or her intent to sacrifice the worldly pleasures and attachments for the sake of this highest purpose. Only a few managed to pass this testing stage. They were accepted into the order of initiates and admitted to secret higher knowledge."

"What happened to Atlantis?"

"It was destroyed according to Divine decision, because the positive development of the society ended and its degradation began.

"Thanks to its knowledge, the Atlantean civilization had a significant advantage over other nations of the Earth. There is no doubt that the Atlanteans, upon choosing the 'evil' path, would conquer other nations with time and establish their order, their philosophy among other people. This is why God decided to end the existence of this civilization."

"Why the positive development of the Atlanteans changed to degradation?"

"As I have said already, the life of the society was guided by several people — the leaders among the initiates. Unfortunately, at some point they fall prey to the false feeling of their own omnipotence and perfection. They ceased to go the path of renunciation of the individual 'I' for the sake of mergence with the Higher, United 'I'. They reckoned that now they themselves could decide the destinies of people and the ways of the society development. They did not want to go further — to the Divine Perfection through refusal of 'I' and 'mine' — but having had achieved a certain height indulged in self-exaltation.

"As a result, the life of people lost the Divine component which gave them joy and inspiration for making efforts for the sake of the future Self-realization in God; their unity, based on selfless service to the great cause, was destroyed. Quarrels and squabbles began to occur often among them.

"Then the higher priests were deposed by a person who aspired for absolute power. He was interested only in gaining power by any means.

"And a society ruled by a predatory person produces other predators which begin to fight for the power.

"Thus Atlantis entered dark times and came eventually to destruction."

"How did You avoid death?"

"My Teacher led Me away.

"God sent Me to Africa, where I lived for many years then. In the modern language, it can be called emigration — when one begins everything from scratch, begins a new life on a new place.

"I brought there an invaluable treasure — the spiritual knowledge of Atlantis.

"The tribes inhabiting those lands were to Me like children, to whom I had to show the path of the true development. They knew nothing about the Highest and were concerned only about their everyday needs.

"With the help of miracles I captured their attention and made them listen to Me. Soon they began to view Me as a leader, and I started to unite these tribes — so that they could live and act jointly, with the feeling of commonality, common interest. I imparted to them knowledge and technology which helped to improve their level of life and make it much better as compared to how they lived before.

"And with time, a state with well working structures was formed.

"But a state without a spiritual purpose uniting all people is of no value; it is like a beautiful shell devoid of life.

"After their union and initial development of the society, when people became less obsessed with concerns of providing themselves with food and shelter, I began shifting the emphasis in their minds to the ideas about the future life in the other world, where everyone goes to after the departure from the body.

"I described it to them as moving to a new world where one comes to new life. The well-being in this life is ensured by one's merits accumulated in the life in this world. For example, man will be respected in that new world if here he earned the respect of his neighbors. In the other world he will be provided with everything if in this world he helped other people to provide themselves. Good deeds in this life are fully repaid in that new life to come!

"It is easy to see that this idea of new life, which one has to ensure by good deeds *at present*, worked not only in helping people to go to paradise after disembodiment, but also provided them with good karma for future incarnations.

"… I became the highest adviser among this nation but never elevated Myself over people.

"… As time passed, a natural formation of classes in that society began. The nobility appeared. And then I decided that My Mission is over and it is time to leave that land.

"I chose an heir to Me who was to remain after My departure — a wise and good man. I told people that now it is My turn to move to the new life — to the world where we receive the fruits of our earthly deeds.

"And one day I 'shifted' Myself from the material world — into My present World, into the Abode of *Light*."

"Did You teach esoteric techniques to those people?"

"Of course, among people there were some chosen whom I taught. I also taught people the art of healing."

"Thoth, tell us please what valuable ideas can modern people find in ancient alchemy?"

"There is no much sense in trying to unravel the meaning of the ancient alchemical texts with the mind. The point here is not in the proportion of substances or composition of mixtures, not in the technology of producing the 'philosopher's stone' and gold. One needs to look deeper.

"The alchemical secrets of control over matter, including its transformation, were known to the Great Initiates. But more important is that They had the higher secret knowledge about the structure of the universe and about the Creator of everything existing.

"The outer, material side of alchemy is nothing but a veil hiding the true Knowledge about the Highest from unworthy people. This Knowledge was the basis of all the alchemical wisdom."

"Did You possess this alchemical knowledge in full?"

"Actually, I was the founder of this direction of spiritual development. Unfortunately it degraded with time and was reduced to useless manipulations with chemical substances."

"What is 'philosopher's stone'?"

"It is very simple. The 'philosopher's stone' is produced when you, in the process of working on yourself, grind 'in mortar' your lower self, while all the Higher Knowledge, which you receive, you test by experience and accept as your own. Then it becomes Higher Wisdom and a strong base — that 'philosopher's stone' on which one can construct the entire building of Divine Beingness."

"What is the 'alchemical gold'?"

"It is adept's consciousness that has to turn into the Highest Gold with the help of 'philosopher's stone': the developed and subtle consciousness has to shine with goldish Light, similar to the light of the morning sun. Then such a consciousness can infuse into the Great Central 'Sun' — into the Creator of the entire universe, merge with Him and attain the Immortality, Bliss, Calm, and full Freedom!"

"Will You tell us about Your higher methods of work with consciousness?"

"It is not necessary. You know now that the higher Initiations are given by Divine Teachers only to those ready for this. And all preparatory stages are described clearly and fully in your books and films. All We are glad looking at the fruits of Our common work! The only pity is that so few people can understand and appreciate it now..."

"Where did You incarnate after Egypt?"

"In Assyria.

"In a certain sense, it was even pleasant 'to wear the flesh' again, to come again to the 'dense' world — now with full awareness of own Divinity.

"Sun was the symbol of the Divine to that nation. The goldish shining and purity of the morning sun are remarkable qualities for attuning to them and refining the soul! What qualities should represent a symbol of the Divine if not the qualities of the ideal that souls may aspire to?

"And such qualities are represented by the image of the morning sun: its perfect, unstained purity inside and its shining with the inner light to the world outside, without dividing it on those to whom I want to give my light and on those to whom I do not want to give it. The absence of such a division originating from sympathies and antipathies of the individual self is also one of the qualities of the Divine.

"I was not a great leader among the people of that land. I accepted another role and 'put on the dress of a priest' — to have the possibility to tell people — brightly and openly — about the Divinity.

"… There was also Alexandria — My favorite city; I looked after it. In this city I formed a new culture for the future civilization. I collected there bright minds of that time, formed an atmosphere for exchange of ideas, for intellectual search. It was My 'project'.

"Many scholars from various countries gathered there. And quite naturally they wanted to tell about their new discoveries and ideas, to learn the views of others. Such communication and the spirit of scientific community worked as a powerful catalyst for the development of knowledge. One may say that it was a very early prototype of future international scientific organizations.

"The intellectual aspect of the soul development is very important indeed!

"The growth of a soul is determined, first of all, by soul's accumulating information about everything that surrounds it. In other words, the soul develops through *cognition*. Thanks to its *separateness*, the soul can look at the rest of the Absolute and cognize it — and through this it cognizes Me.

"Thus, by reproducing *in itself* the outer the soul, in essence, reproduces *in itself* the image of the multidimensional universe.

"Then it comes to full Mergence.

"Thus a great number of individualities infuse into the One and Whole Awareness of My Infinite Greatness.

"Hence the driving force behind all the development is the inner impulse to *cognition*."

Cairo

Visiting once a foreign town, we came upon a square where stood a Giant Mahadouble of a Divine Teacher Whom we had never met before.

Of course, we asked first what is His name.

He answered:

"My name is Cairo. The word *Cairo* in Atlantis meant *Earth*: Earth as a living planet![30]

"Atlantis was My 'earth'. From Atlantis this name came to the capital of Egypt.

"Since that time I have never incarnated again."

"Were You a priest in Atlantis?"

"I was one of the five Atlantean rulers. There was a group of five rulers-elders, and I was its leader. I rep-

---

[30] In Arabic there is a similar word *qahirah* meaning 'victorious'. Among historians there is an opinion that the city name Cairo originated from this word.

resented the temporal power which possessed spiritual knowledge.

"The history of civilization, the history of the spiritual life on the Earth is more ancient than modern people think it is. Atlantis was not the beginning of the spiritual development on the Earth. It was only one of big stages. Many times the configuration of the oceans and continents changed, and the *Dweller of the Depths* created every time new conditions for growth and development of souls.

"The story of Atlantis can be useful for modern people. Adler, Thoth, and I can tell everything important of it."

"How one can avoid falling into non-adequate fantasizing about Atlantis? There are plenty of examples of mediums communicating inaccurate information!"

"One should not try to communicate the information which is above one's intellectual abilities of comprehension. Otherwise higher knowledge and information gets expressed in primitive words and images, and this results in its distortion similar to religious myths of undeveloped nations, which reflect in tales and legends some realities of the past in a non-recognizable form.

"But let Me begin narration. I want to tell you that part of knowledge and information which you can comprehend and which should be conveyed to the people of the Earth now.

"In Atlantis there existed a great civilization. The leaders of that society possessed the highest spiritual knowledge.

"The leaders of society, who direct the spiritual growth of people, bear great responsibility. Even a smallest deviation from the principles of Divine Love and Selflessness may become a turning to the abyss where one loses the connection with the Creator! Exactly this happened in Atlantis (the power was taken over by selfish people), and God decided to end this period of the development of consciousnesses on the Earth — to destroy Atlantis.

"… I will tell you also about the *Temple*.

"The image of temple is not a human invention. The *Temple* is a Divine structure in the multidimensional organism of a living planet. Its most close equivalent is *Shambala* — i.e. the place inside the planet where Divine Consciousnesses live in the Highest spatial dimension; it has an exit to the *Boundless Ocean* of the Creator's Consciousness.

"The *Temple* is the epicenter of creation of life on the planet. It is the place where abide Those Who supervise the development of life on this islet of the Divine Creation.

"The *Temple* has an 'exit' and an 'entrance'. This Divine structure in the multidimensional organism of the Earth is as real as the kundalini in the multidimensional organism of man. In the Atmic component of the human organism there is memory about the past incarnations — so is with the *Temple*: by submerging into the *Temple* one can learn about important episodes of the planet's life. For example, one can read the pages of the history of Atlantis — to learn about the Atlanteans of Spirit: about Adler, Thoth, and Others, who 'interwove' Themselves (as Consciousnesses) into the life of the planet — for the sake of the development of consciousnesses growing on the Earth.

"Originally, all rulers of Atlantis throughout centuries had the 'keys to the *Temple*'; that is, they lived coming out as Brahmanic Consciousnesses from the *Temple* and had the ability to immerse and to dissolve their Divine Individualities in the Ocean of the Creator's Consciousness. In this way the Atlantean civilization was guided and developed.

"Pyramids and other earthly temples are but a reflection of the *Temple* where the initiation of souls was performed.

"Every planet is created as densification of the energy of Consciousness up to the material plane. Then there starts the process of the development of life in material carriers.

"The souls incarnated in Atlantis had gone through incarnations on other planets. They were well advanced souls but not Divine yet. The majority of the Atlanteans lived being aware of themselves as souls rather than material bodies. They enjoyed the intense feelings of the life in a physical body. The power of such feelings is much more impressive than paradisiacal life without a body. This power of feelings was delightful for souls who lived for a long time in the non-incarnate state. They lived in the states close to Samadhi, and one could call it a paradise on the Earth. For many of them it was the last or prior to the last incarnation, and the conditions were quite favorable for attainment of the Divinity by them.

"The Atlantean educational system included the skills of psychic self-regulation, the knowledge about the structure of the multidimensional universe, ethics and different kinds of art, creativity in science and technology, which were developed to a high level.

"For those who had chose for themselves realization of the highest meaning of life — cognition of the Creator — there were spiritual initiations. This type of education was closed, esoteric; it was accessible only to those who understood the higher meaning and purpose of their lives. Among their Teachers there were Divine Souls possessing material bodies, which are used as *instruments* of Divine Creativity in such cases.

"The long existence of the Atlantean civilization allowed many paradisiacal souls to complete the cycle of evolution and to merge into the Creator. They did not need to incarnate again any more.

"As for the Atlanteans who, upon receiving physical bodies, chose the path of material self-gratification, through sex in particular, — through them new human races were created. They were races of people who grew then as consciousnesses on this planet — new 'shoots' of young souls to go through the long process of evolution.

"Such a mixture of races resulted in many legends and myths about gods in different nations. Elisabeth Haich described very precisely that in that time on the Earth there were races of people with very different level of development of consciousnesses and bodies. The mixture of these races through sex and birth of offspring accelerated significantly the process of evolution.

"As for Those achieved Mergence with Creator — They have never incarnated again, except for a few Who chose to take care of the new generations of people. Among the latter are Those wished together with Adler to guide people on the Path of self-realization and cognition of the *Divine Oneness*. They incarnated again and again bringing to people the knowledge about the Highest. All this is a very long process taking millennia; you will have a chance to participate in it too."

Nikifor

To the first meeting with Divine Nikifor on His favorite *place of power* in the forest we were prepared by Divine Sulia.

"Where did Nikifor incarnate last time?"

She shows the Pacific region to the northwest of Australia, on islands close to it.

"Now it is His turn to work with you!

"You informed people in this region about your knowledge through the Internet; it was not by chance. It was necessary that in this region too people learn about you."

"The name *Nikifor* is of Greek origin?"

"Not exactly. It became Greek, Byzantine later. This name is international; it must not be related to a certain nation."

… And now we are standing on the edge of a large forest glade overgrown with young birches and pines. Visiting Nikifor, we are standing inside His giant Mahadouble, composed of Living Divine Light.

The most wonderful thing here is that upon coming out from the forest to the glade one finds oneself… in the expanse of non-material *ocean*! The other reality of beingness becomes visible here to the eyes of a refined consciousness: oceanic expanse with calls of soaring gulls and a *white sailboat*. It is also the Ocean of Divine Light! Most tender and pure transparency of Its Depths, universal Calm, and Harmony of Divine Beingness give you the feeling of the highest bliss and serenity of existence in great *Oneness* of Divine Souls!

"Tell us please how did You attain such Mastery — You can manifest so easily on the Earth the

Depths of the Ocean of the Primordial Consciousness?"

"I grew on the oceanic coast. In the oceanic expanse I cognized the Divine Wisdom! My Love grew in freedom, in expanse, — and there were no bounds to it!

"I cognized God orienting Myself not to Individual Manifestations of the Creator — Divine Teachers, but to the Absolute: to the Universal Multidimensional Organism with Its Base in the primordial loka — in the Heart of the Absolute. You are luckier! You have so many Divine Friends-Teachers, and I am one of Them," laughs Nikifor.

"Tell us please about Yourself: it is so valuable to know one more possibility of cognition of God! How did You attain the Divinity? And when?"

"It was long ago… at the time of Atlantis. Later I incarnated once more on islands in the Australian region… They were very large islands; later they submerged into the ocean. There was a School of buddhi yoga of a very high level, similar to the Egyptian School of Ptahotep. First, I was a student and then a Teacher of this School."

"In what spiritual traditions did You work?"

"By God we called the United Highest Consciousness. My Mission was to teach the students, who had achieved the needed level, to be established in the status of the Ocean of the Primordial Consciousness. In other words, My Mission was to teach Mahatmas to be the Ocean of Paramatman!

"I will teach you the same too.

"Listen now to My directions on meditation:

"One has to learn to live being constantly aware of oneself as the Only Existing Self — the Self of God!

"I am the Bliss, Tenderness, and Power of the Creator!

"I am Love! I am Light! I am Blissful Beingness!

"Try to feel this, immersing yourselves into Me-Universal, Me-the-*Ocean*...

"Feel that there is only My Anahata — the *Ocean* of Me... Or feel Me as an Infinite *Wave*... And there is only the Infinity the Creator...

"And the completely purified body can be likened to a slit: through it you can perceive the material plane from the *Ocean*, while you are one with the *Ocean*..."

"But how can we learn to be always in Mergence?"

"How does one master every next stage?...

"The Ocean of the Creator is the Subtlest... Gently and softly, on the background of dissolving Calm — learn to BE Me!

"The state of the *Ocean* is soft Calm, the Bliss of Giving Love...

"If you cannot manage to move to the necessary *depth* at once, recall the meditative methods which you know: for example,

"... I am always and everywhere! The entire Infinity of Me — of the Universal *Ocean* of the Creator — is separated from the Creation only by the finest membrane of the 'Curtain', which can be crossed easily in any point of space. *Love* easily permeates through it into the *Ocean* of Me, as if being attracted by the Universal Magnet. The identical merge into *One* — thus works the *Law of attraction*.

"You are identical to Me! You flow into the *Deepest Layer* and remain *There* being connected, fastened by the awareness: 'Waters of *love* which have infused into the *Ocean* are inseparable from the *Ocean*, and this is I!'

"But this is not all to it.

"With your hands of consciousness — perceive the Infinity of Yourself-the-*Ocean*...

"There is only the *Ocean*... This is what Godcenteredness is.

"This means accustoming oneself to be the Heart of the Absolute: the United Higher Self, the United *Ocean* of You, Me, Everyone...!

"The one who has known the *Ocean of Love* aspires to It again and again!

"By submerging into Its transparency, one blends with It!

"By giving oneself, forgetting oneself, one dissolves in It!

"A heart which has encompassed the *Ocean* becomes the *Ocean*!

"A soul which has become the *Ocean* lives the life of the *Ocean*!"

"... Nikifor! The image of a *white sailboat* on the surface of the *Ocean* — what is its meaning?"

"We had light small vessels with white sails. On such a vessel the Messengers of the School went to every new spiritual seeker who, being a mature soul, addressed God with a request of receiving the Great Initiation and of being taught to help people.

"Such a request was always clearly perceivable to the Members of our School — and a sailboat was sent to such a seeker. Our messengers in white clothes went directly to that person, easily finding him or her in a ruler's palace or in a pauper's hut. They repeated to that person verbatim the words of the appeal about the Great Initiation and offered him or her to go to the Path. And then the new seeker went together with them to the vessel and came to the School to learn there the higher steps of the *Path of soul*.

"If that person wavered, being astonished by so prompt 'material' response to his or her appeal, the Messengers left to the shore and the sail waited there for three days… During these days the person could make the decision.

"Usually in these days, many people came to the Divine vessel, and our Messengers told them the words of truth, gave simple and clear precepts, healed them… All this remained in the memory of people as legends about God's 'descended from Heavens'.

"The School was situated on an island and was not associated with any state. It was autonomous and independent of the outer world.

"In the beginning of studying in the School, much attention was paid to the purity of the energy structures of the body (on the Atmic level of subtlety) and to the absolute control of the consciousness over the functions of the organism — both in the emotional-volitional sphere and on the physical level, up to control over the heart rate, respiration rate, functioning of the internal organs. Such psycho-physical exercises were taught to all beginners, independent of the age. Along with preparation of the body, one was taught the truths about the structure of the multidimensional universe, the meaning of human life, the nature of God.

"Then the students entered the stage of buddhi yoga. It was similar to yours; just the level of the consciousnesses of the beginners was much higher, and our initial steps were not 'the first grade of school', but 'the first grade of university', drawing an analogy with your contemporary world.

"... How can one perform actions on the Earth and at the same time remain in Mergence with Me? The main point here is *from where* your action originates: from Me or from the lower self and what the *purpose* of the action is.

"By his actions, man can either construct 'nest' for his lower self — or do My Will.

"Conscious actions, which originate from My Intent and realize it, can never enslave you! On the contrary, they strengthen your Mergence with Me!"

"But what about feeding the body, household duties, etc?"

"Distinguish the cycling of matter in the world of prakriti — and actions related to My Life.

"That what you say about is just the cycling in the world of prakriti. Distinguish from it the actions that enter the world of prakriti from Me and that are aimed outside of this world.

"You must live not only by the cycling of matter in the world of prakriti, but — with your aspirations and actions — you must live outside it!

"... It is wrong to think that God does not care about your material problems — this is not true.

"I simply have no problems or failures in the material world. And you, too, if you are *One* with Me, — will have no problems.

"When you are not with Me, you miss the possibility: wrongly chosen time, ill-timed action... This results in wasting of time and efforts.

"Always feel the way which I open for you! Walking it, you arrive to the destination in time, and there — everything is ready for your coming: it is Me taking care about you.

"But if you start a journey without paying heed to My signs, then on the finish you may experience bad luck or total failure. In other words, you encounter there your karma."

Odin

"Odin, will You please relate about Your Path? How did You become Divine?"

"… It was long time ago… I was a Varangian, a captain of a merchant sailing ship… Rocks, winds, severe storms of the northern seas…

"I learned to steer My ship, aligning My will with the elements of the ocean. I learned to stand firmly on the deck dropping out from under the feet, to unite the power of My arms, holding guy ropes or the steering oar, the will of the ocean and the will of My crew…

"Most of the time I was in the ocean. And I learned to love the far, longed-for land — to love it like a fortune, like a continuation of life which is given as a reward for the strength, courage, and fortitude…

"Thanks to this, I mastered that *power of soul* which is capable of making its way knowing that there are storms, the destiny, God…

"… I never 'prayed' to Him… I knew that He holds in His Hands the steering oar of My life, and that if I turn to the wrong direction, He has a right to take this life… I felt Him — as I felt the elements of the ocean and wind, as I felt My ship and My friends, who entrusted their lives to Me. In storm and in calm, when moving forward requires no less skills than surviving in tempest, — I felt Him. ... I trusted Him, but never 'prayed' to Him...

"... Then, I came to know *love* — tenderness and subtlety of love, which turned out to be above *power*..."

Odin showed an image of a beautiful young woman with long light hair and great tenderness in the depth of her eyes... This image was filled with soft calm...

He did not say anything more about her...

As the ocean keeps a pearl in its translucent depths, even so this love is kept in the depths of this Divine Soul...

His might and power transformed then into love and tenderness...

"After that, I cognized the *Oneness*."

He showed an image of Himself walking in morning sunlight. White long curly hair and beard, wisdom of elder, power of mature man, and carriage of youth — all these had united in His body... Divinity — like morning sunlight — was streaming from His eyes. The Calm of the *Ocean* had become His Essence.

Now He identified Himself with the *body* not more than with the earth which He walked, not more than with the morning light or with the soft mist dancing above smooth surface of lakes. He identified Himself with the *body* not more than with the calmness of granite rocks towering over glassy pellucid waters, not more than with tall pines reaching for the sky... And He was all this — not more than He was the fathomless Ocean of Light in the *Depth beneath*... He was *Everything* — at one and the same time...

… Then Odin showed His present appearance, in which we saw Him for the first time. He was like a Mountain rising from the Infinite Ocean of the Primordial Consciousness and opening with Itself an entrance into the Depths of the multidimensional Creation. His Face with white curly hair resembling oceanic waves was the top of the *Mountain*. And His Hands below the surface of the Ocean supported with the Palms all living beings in the Creation, filling them with power — with power to grow, to develop, to love, to be…

"What can You advice us concerning how we should live?"

"How to live? — Live with Me, from Me… And sow the seeds of My Love and Knowledge! Then people will go to the Light… — not immediately, not everyone, but there will be sprouts!…"

"How to sow?"

"Gently and softly, as a sower: he walks over the field, — and in a wide gesture the hand throws the seeds… Then rain waters the soil… And the sun warms it… And patient time goes by…

"There will be sprouts!

"Scientists working for God! Scientists studying Me, serving Me, sacrificing themselves for the sake of Me! I am proud of you; I am proud, in particular, that I helped you to find and cognize Me!

"Your scientific group, at present, is the only one on the Earth successful in studying Me. You are not only a leading scientific group on the planet, but a unique one in this respect!

"I congratulate you on this!"

"Odin, tell us please: what does one need to do in order to master being in complete and permanent *Oneness*?"

"The foundation of *Oneness* is Love! This is a very important meditation: when the entire Absolute is My Anahata, My Heart; when I contain Everything in My Heart, in My Love; when I pervade everything, control everything; when I am Everything; when everything is pervaded with My Divine Love — every single atom!

"Yamamata told you: from outside one sees the Sun 'rising' over the ocean, but inside there is only *Ocean*…

"And I am telling you: everything, absolutely everything, that you see from outside, is One inside: the Boundless Ocean of the Creator — *Oneness* of the Whole! Everything rests on Him; everything is pervaded with the Transparent Component of His *Depths*!

"Everything is *One*, and in this *Oneness* you may gain omniscience, omnipresence, and the ability to control everything: small particles of Yourself inside Yourself-Whole…

"And let Me repeat that one can cognize the *Oneness* of everything only through Love!"

* * *

"… I am going to tell you about the Aesir, as They are called in Scandinavian legends and sagas. They were the Atlanteans Who assumed responsibility for the destiny of people on the Earth after the destruction of Atlantis.

"They were not many. But Their life span was much longer than that of other people living on the Earth at that time. They lived in the body for 300-500 years; it was normal for the Atlanteans. People remembered Them as Gods coming down from Heavens and ruling the Earth. They would come to the Earth again and again, taking mortal women for wives, and this would bind Them to the material plane… Yet in every incarnation, They would bring the new mortal body to the Fullness of the Divine Awareness… As Bight Suns of Divine Consciousness, They guided the life on the Earth…

"I was One of Them…

"For many lives I came to the Creation and every time connected the embodied part of Myself-Consciousness with the Consciousness of the Creator.

"I became like a Mountain: its base is the Infinite Ocean of the Creator and its sides are this material world. I became 'rooted' so firmly that managed to finish with complete Mergence even My Varangian incarnation in the world where there was no knowledge about the Creator!

"… None of Those Great Souls counted on a quick success in spiritual transformation of people on the Earth. One cannot impart higher knowledge to people who just begin their evolutionary path in human bodies. Awareness grows slowly in a series of many incarnations."

"Do people need to know that which You describe? After all, the majority of them will take all this as fairy tales, which have no documentary evidence…"

"People do need to know it! This will expand the horizons, switch their thinking from little mundane concerns — to a broad look into the depth of the history of civilization, into the meaning of human life… This will make them to ponder about the evolution of consciousnesses in the universe, about the means of the

Divine control over this process. People's look will be directed not down at their feet; they will look farther, broader, deeper. The future will become open for creativity; every person aware of the meaning of our existence will be able to take part in creating this future!

"You may note that the modern youth is very interested in fantasy, fairy tales, myths where adventures of people and sorcerers open prospects of life of consciousnesses, not just bodies... This is one of the means for redirecting the interest of youth to the world of Spirit.

"If you tell to the public about the Reality which I am describing now and which is much more interesting than fairy tales, then it may help to infuse a new current into the thinking of people.

"You should create a website on this subject. It may include the materials about Yamamata, Huang Di, Nikifor, Assyris and His schools, Pythagoras and, of course, about Adler. Some new material is going to be added soon; so the site can be ready by spring."

But everything we do is not popular among people: they are interested only in how to become happy, healthy, rich..."

"Fine! Your next film may be *The Art of Being Happy!*"

* * *

"I have guided many Finns to the Abode of the Creator! You are the first Russian spiritual warriors to come to Me — and I am very glad to meet you!

"But I ask you not to forget about the affliction of the Finnish nation that suffered guiltlessly during the World War II...

"Service! Throughout the whole planet you have to arrange camps for teaching children and youth — 'miniashrams'!

"Inform through the Internet pedagogues of different countries… Engage in this work all your human resources! Republish the books! The book *Spiritual Work with Children* has to be translated into other languages!"

"The knowledge, which you received, has to be made available to all people of the Earth!"

Bibliography

1. Antonov V.V. — Classics of Spiritual Philosophy and the Present, "New Atlanteans", "Lulu.com", 2008.

2. Antonov V.V. — Ecopsychology, "New Atlanteans", "Lulu.com", 2008.

Our video films:

1. *Immersion into Harmony of Nature. The Way to Paradise.* (Slideshow), 90 minutes (on CD or DVD).
2. *Spiritual Heart.* 70 minutes (on DVD).
3. *Sattva (Harmony, Purity).* 60 minutes (on DVD).
4. *Sattva of Mists.* 75 minutes (on DVD).
5. *Sattva of Spring.* 90 minutes (on DVD).
6. *Art of Being Happy.* 42 minutes (on DVD).
7. *Keys to the Secrets of Life. Achievement of Immortality.* 38 minutes (on DVD).
8. *Bhakti Yoga.* 47 minutes (on DVD).
9. *Kriya Yoga.* 40 minutes (on DVD).
10. *Practical Ecopsychology.* 60 minutes (on DVD).
11. *Yoga of Krishna.* 80 minutes (on DVD).

You may order our books and films at Lulu e-store: http://stores.lulu.com/spiritualheart

You can also download for free our video films, screensavers, printable calendars, etc from the site: www.spiritual-art.info

See on the site www.swami-center.org our books, photo gallery, and other materials in different languages.

Cover design by
Ekaterina Smirnova